Korea Travel J

Name: _____

Travel dates: _____

Places visited: _____

_____

TUTTLE Publishing

Tokyo | Rutland, Vermont | Singapore

Seoul's Top Sites

Jingwansa Temple
Yeonsinnae Station (subway Line 3)
then take shuttle bus

Bukchon Hanok Village
Anguk Station (subway Line 3)

Itaewon Entertainment District
Itaewon, Noksapyeong and Hanganjin
stations (subway Line 6)

Gyeongbokgung
Palace

N Seou

Lotte
World

Yeojwacheon
Stream

Gyeongbokgung Palace
Gyeongbokgung Station (subway Line 3)

Jogyesa Temple

Island

Seoraksan

dong

Bukchon Hanok

Insadong Shopping Area
Anguk Station (subway Line 3)

K-Star Road
Apgujeong Rodeo Station exit 2
(Bundang Line)

Myeongdong Underground
Shopping Center
Myeongdong Station
(subway Line 4)

Gwangjang Market
Jongno 5-ga Station (subway Line 1)

Gyeongbokgung Palace

This ancient palace was built in 1395.

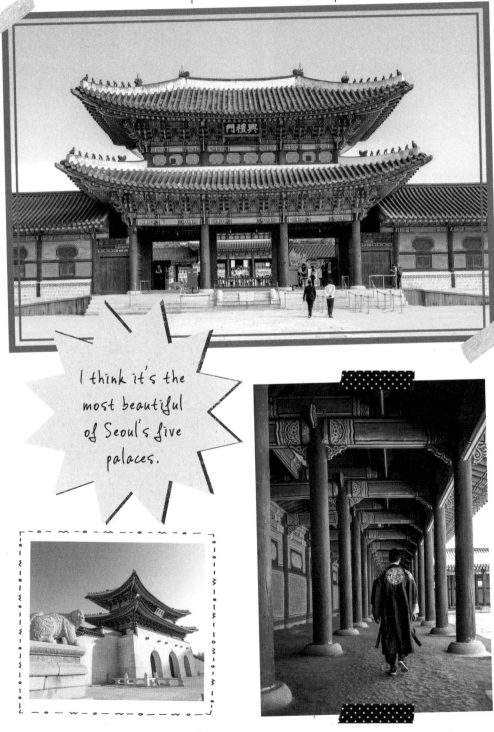

I think it's the most beautiful of Seoul's five palaces.

N Seoul Tower

Located on Namsam Mountain in the middle of Seoul,
it's one of the highest places in the city.

Take the cable car to the top of the mountain
and enjoy the amazing views!

It's a place
of romantic
pilgrimage, where
couples leave
padlocks to declare
eternal love.

Bukchon Hanok Village

This traditional village shows what life was like 600 years ago.

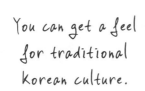

You can get a feel for traditional Korean culture.

Jingwansa Temple

his Buddhist temple is hundreds of years ld. It's surrounded by beautiful parkland, a really peaceful break from the city.

Cheonggyecheon Stream

This city center stream was hidden for years,
but is now a popular 7 mile (11 km) long recreation space.

Gwangjang Market

One of South korea's largest traditional markets.

We had great street food there!

Itaewon Entertainment District

Seoul's most cosmopolitan neighborhood. Great for souvenirs and leather goods.

The area is packed with trendy bars and restaurants.

Insadong Shopping Area

Insadong is the best place to buy traditional crafts.

There are lots of really cool cafés.

★ Idol Spotting! ★

The JYP agency manages top k-pop groups. Hang out at a nearby cafe, like **The Street** (125-18 Cheongdam-dong) and you might see your favorite idol!

Yujeong Sikdang is a favorite restaurant of BTS (14 Dosan-daero 28-gil, Gangnam-gu).

K-Star Road in the Apgujeong Rodeo neighborhood has various entertainment agencies. It's a great place for idol spotting!

Myeongdong Underground Shopping Center

I bought lots of k-pop and k-drama merchandise at this shopping mall.

The DMZ

We took a tour to the Demilitarized Zone, which marks the border between North and South korea.

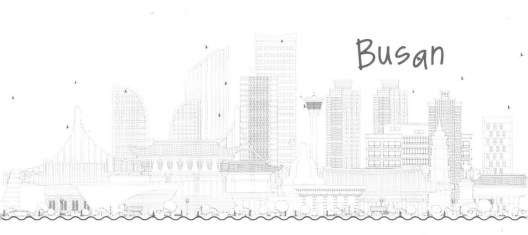

Busan

Korea's bustling second city in the south of the Korean peninsula. It's a busy port, with great beaches.

Jeju Island

We had wonderful beach holiday here!

We also saw spectacular mountains and waterfalls.

.

Useful Korean Words and Phrases

Hello.	안녕하세요.	**Annyeonghaseyo.**
Nice to meet you.	처음 뵙겠습니다.	**Cheoeum boepgessseupnida.**
Nice to see you.	만나서 반갑습니다.	**Mannaseo bangapseupnida.**
Please come in.	들어오세요.	**Deureooseyo.**
Welcome!	환영합니다!	**Hwanyeonghapnida!**
It's been a while.	오랜만이에요.	**Olaenmanieyo.**
How have you been?	잘 지냈어요?	**Jal jinaesseoyo?**
I've been well.	잘 지냈어요.	**Jal jinaesseoyo.**
Thank you.	감사합니다.	**Gamsahapnida.**
Excuse me.	실례합니다.	**Sillyehapnida.**
I am sorry.	죄송합니다.	**Joesonghapnida.**
It's ok.	괜찮습니다.	**Gwaenchanseupnida.**
yes	네	**ne**
no	아니요	**aniyo**
Congratulations!	축하합니다!	**Chukhahapnida!**
Goodbye (to person leaving).	안녕히 가세요.	**Annyeonghi gaseyo.**
Goodbye (to person staying).	안녕히 계세요.	**Annyeonghi gyeseyo.**
See you later.	나중에 뵙겠습니다.	**Najunge boepgessseupnida.**

personal information	개인정보	**gaeinjeongbo**
address	주소	**juso**
age	나이	**nai**
birthday	생일	**saengil**
cellphone number	휴대전화 번호	**hyudaejeonhwa beonho**
date of birth	생년월일	**saengnyeonwolil**
driver's license	운전면허증	**unjeonmyeonheojeung**
hometown	고향	**gohyang**
ID card	신분증	**sinbunjeung**
marriage	결혼	**gyeolhon**
nationality	국적	**gukjeok**
occupation	직업	**jikeop**
passport	여권	**yeogwon**
phone number	전화 번호	**jeonhwa beonho**
school	학교	**hakkyo**
single	미혼	**mihon**
married	기혼	**gihon**
divorced	이혼	**ihon**

Transport

transport	교통	**gyotong**		road	도로	**doro**
airplane	비행기	**bihaenggi**		street	길	**gil**
bicycle	자전거	**jajeongeo**		subway	지하철	**jihacheol**
boat	배	**bae**		taxi	택시	**taeksi**
bus	버스	**beoseu**		train	기차	**gicha**
car	자동차	**jadongcha**		truck	트럭	**teureok**
car accident	교통사고	**gyotongsago**				

Around Town

airport	공항	**gonghang**		Korea town	한인타운	**hanintaun**
art gallery	미술관	**misulgwan**		library	도서관	**doseogwan**
bank	은행	**eunhaeng**		museum	박물관	**bakmulgwan**
baseball park	야구장	**yagujang**		park	공원	**gongwon**
beach	바닷가	**badatkka**		pharmacy	약국	**yakkuk**
café	카페	**kape**		post office	우체국	**ucheguk**
church	교회	**gyohoe**		restaurant	식당	**sikdang**
department store	백화점	**baekhwajeom**		restroom	화장실	**hwajangsil**
embassy	대사관	**daesagwan**		school	학교	**hakgyo**
gym	체육관	**cheyukgwan**		station	역	**yeok**
hair salon	미용실	**miyongsil**		store	가게	**gage**
hospital	병원	**byeongwon**		swimming pool	수영장	**suyeongjang**
hotel	호텔	**hotel**		theater	극장	**geukjang**
karaoke room	노래방	**noraebang**		temple	절	**jeol**

Directions

direction	방향 / 위치	**banghyang / wichi**		center	중간	**jungkan**
front	앞	**ap**		between	사이 / 가운데	**sai / gaunde**
back	뒤	**dwi**		outside	밖	**bak**
right	오른쪽	**oreunjjok**		next to	옆	**yeop**
left	왼쪽	**oenjjok**		around	주위	**juwi**
go straight	직진하세요	**jikjinhaseyo**		vicinity	근처	**geuncheo**
above; on	위	**wi**		north	북	**buk**
below	밑	**mit**		south	남	**nam**
under	아래	**area**		east	동	**dong**
inside	안	**an**		west	서	**seo**

Question & Answer Words

what	뭐 / 무엇	**mwo / mueot**		which one?	어느?	**eoneu?**
when	언제	**eonje**		who	누구	**nugu**
where	어디	**eodi**		why	왜	**woe**

In a Restaurant

English	Korean	Romanization
Welcome!	어서 오세요.	**Eoseo oseyo!**
How many people?	몇 분이세요?	**Myeot buniseyo?**
Please come this way.	이쪽으로 오세요.	**Ijjokeuro oseyo.**
Please sit here.	여기 앉으세요.	**Yeogi anjeuseyo.**
Here is the menu.	메뉴가 있어요.	**Menyuga isseoyo.**
Would you like to order?	주문하시겠어요?	**Jumunhasigetsseoyo?**
. . . , please.	. . . 주세요.	**. . . , juseyo.**
I will enjoy the food!	잘 먹겠습니다!	**Jal mukgetsseumnida!**
I enjoyed the food.	잘 먹었습니다.	**Jal meogeosseumnida.**
The check, please.	계산해 주세요.	**Gyesanhae juseyo.**
The receipt, please.	영수증 주세요.	**Yeongsujeung juseyo.**
Please come again.	또 오세요.	**Tto oseyo.**

A Restaurant Menu

English	Korean	Romanization
food	음식	**eumsik**
Korean food	한국 음식	**hankuk eumsik**
beef short rib	갈비	**galbi**
beef short rib soup	갈비탕	**galbitang**
bibimbap	비빔밥	**bibimbap**
braised beef short rib	갈비찜	**galbijjim**
bulgogi	불고기	**bulgogi**
deep-fried dumplings	만두	**mandu**
fried rice	볶음밥	**bokkeumbap**
gimbap	김밥	**gimbap**
green onion pancake	파전	**pajeon**
kimchi	김치	**gimchi**
kimchi pancake	김치전	**gimchijeon**
kimchi stew	김치찌개	**gimchijjigae**
noodles	국수	**guksu**
noodles (cold)	물냉면	**mulnaengmyeon**
noodles (spicy)	비빔냉면	**bibimnaengmyeon**
pork belly	삼겹살	**samkyeopsal**
ramen	라면	**lamyeon**
raw fish	회	**hoe**
rice (cooked)	밥	**bap**
seafood pancake	해물파전	**haemulpajeon**
side dish	반찬	**banchan**
soft tofu stew	순두부찌개	**sundubujjigae**
soybean-paste stew	된장찌개	**doenjangjjigae**
spicy beef stew	육개장	**yukgaejang**

A Restaurant Menu (cont'd)

stir-fried rice cakes	떡볶이	**tteokbokki**
stir-fried spicy pork	제육볶음	**jeyukbokkeum**
stir-fried spicy squid	오징어볶음	**ojingeobokkeum**
stone bibimbap	돌솥 비빔밥	**tolsot bibimbap**

Drinks

alcohol	술	**sul**	milk	우유	**uyu**
beer	맥주	**maekju**	soda	탄산음료	**tansaneumryo**
beverage	음료수	**eumryosu**	soju	소주	**soju**
cinammon punch	수정과	**sujeonggwa**	sweet rice punch	식혜	**sikhae**
coffee	커피	**keopi**	tea	차	**cha**
juice	주스	**juseu**	water	물	**mul**
green tea	녹차	**nokcha**	wine	와인	**wain**
makgeolli	막걸리	**makgeolli**			

Money

bankbook	통장	**tongjang**	price	가격	**gagyeok**
cash	현금	**hyeongeum**	purse; wallet	지갑	**jigap**
check	수표	**supyo**	receipt	영수증	**yeongsujeung**
coin	동전	**dongjeon**	stamp	도장	**dojang**
discount	할인	**halin**	won	원	**won**
dollar	달러	**dalleo**	yen	엔	**en**
euro	유로	**yuro**	to borrow	빌리다	**billida**
fee; bill	요금	**yogeum**	to lend	빌려주다	**billyeojuda**
money	돈	**don**	to pay	내다	**naeda**

IT & Social Media

app	앱	**aeb**	password	패스워드	**paeseuwodeu**
computer	컴퓨터	**keompyuteo**	phone	전화	**jeonhwa**
data	데이터	**deiteo**	search	검색	**geomsaek**
download	다운로드	**daunrodeu**	selfie	셀카	**selka**
email	이메일	**imeil**	social media	소셜미디어	**sosyeol midieo**
Facebook	페이스북	**peiseubuk**	smartphone	스마트폰	**seumateupon**
file	파일	**pail**	software	소프트웨어	**sopeuteuweeo**
Instagram	인스타그램	**inseu ta geulaem**	tablet	테블렛	**taebeullet**
Internet	인터넷	**inteonet**	technology	기술	**gisul**
laptop	노트북	**noteubuk**	text message	문자	**munja**
login	로그인	**logeuin**	Twitter	트위터	**teuwiteo**
logout	로그아웃	**logeuaut**	Tweet	트윗	**teuwit**
netizen	네티즌	**netijeun**	YouTube	유투브	**yutubeu**

"Books to Span the East and West"

Tuttle Publishing was founded in 1832 in the small New England town of Rutland, Vermont [USA]. Our core values remain as strong today as they were then—to publish best-in-class books which bring people together one page at a time. In 1948, we established a publishing outpost in Japan—and Tuttle is now a leader in publishing English-language books about the arts, languages and cultures of Asia. The world has become a much smaller place today and Asia's economic and cultural influence has grown. Yet the need for meaningful dialogue and information about this diverse region has never been greater. Over the past seven decades, Tuttle has published thousands of books on subjects ranging from martial arts and paper crafts to language learning and literature—and our talented authors, illustrators, designers and photographers have won many prestigious awards. We welcome you to explore the wealth of information available on Asia at **www.tuttlepublishing.com**.

Published by Tuttle Publishing, an imprint of Periplus Editions (HK) Ltd.

www.tuttlepublishing.com

Copyright ©2023 by Periplus Editions (HK) Ltd. All photos Shutterstock.

Library of Congress Catalog-in-Publication Data in progress

ISBN 978-0-8048-5612-6

First edition, 2023
26 25 24 23   5 4 3 2 1

Printed in China   2211CM

Distributed by

North America, Latin America & Europe
Tuttle Publishing
364 Innovation Drive
North Clarendon,
VT 05759-9436 U.S.A.
Tel: 1 (802) 773-8930; Fax: 1 (802) 773-6993
info@tuttlepublishing.com
www.tuttlepublishing.com

Asia Pacific
Berkeley Books Pte. Ltd.
3 Kallang Sector #04-01
Singapore 349278
Tel: (65) 6741-2178; Fax: (65) 6741-2179
inquiries@periplus.com.sg
www.tuttlepublishing.com